U.S. Public Policy toward Network Industries

Lawrence J. White

AEI-Brookings Joint Center for Regulatory Studies

WASHINGTON, D.C.

1999

The author would like to thank Robert W. Hahn, David E. M. Sappington, and the participants at the AEI seminar on Reviving Regulatory Reform for helpful comments on an earlier version of this volume.

ISBN 0-8447-7140-6

1 3 5 7 9 10 8 6 4 2

Contents

Foreword

This volume is one in a series commissioned by the AEI-Brookings Joint Center for Regulatory Studies to contribute to the continuing debate over regulatory reform. The series will address several fundamental issues in regulation, including the design of effective reforms, the impact of proposed reforms on the public, and the political and institutional forces that affect reform.

Many forms of regulation have grown dramatically in recent decades—especially in the areas of environment, health, and safety. Moreover, expenditures in those areas are likely to continue to grow faster than the rate of government spending. Yet, the economic impact of regulation receives much less scrutiny than direct, budgeted government spending. We believe that policymakers need to rectify that imbalance.

The federal government has made substantial progress in reforming economic regulation—principally by deregulating prices and reducing entry barriers in specific industries. For example, over the past two decades consumers have realized major gains from the deregulation of transportation services. Still, policymakers can achieve significant additional gains from fully deregulating other industries, such as telecommunications and electricity.

While deregulating specific industries has led to substantial economywide gains, the steady rise in social regulation—which includes not only environmental, health, and safety standards but many other government-imposed rights and benefits—has had mixed results. Entrepreneurs increasingly face an assortment of employer mandates and legal liabilities that dictate decisions about products, pay-rolls, and personnel practices. Several scholars have questioned the wisdom of that expansion in social regulation. Some regulations, such as the phaseout of lead in gasoline, have been quite successful, while others, such as the requirement for safety caps on aspirin bottles, have led to increased risks. As those regulatory activities grow, so does the need to consider their implications more carefully.

We do not take the view that all regulation is bad or that all proposed reforms are good. We should judge regulations by their individual benefits and costs, which in the past have varied widely. Similarly, we should judge reform proposals on the basis of their likely benefits and costs. The important point is that, in an era when regulation appears to impose very substantial costs in the form of higher consumer prices and lower economic output, carefully weighing the likely benefits and costs of rules and reform proposals is essential for defining an appropriate scope for regulatory activity.

The debates over regulatory policy have often been highly partisan and ill-informed. We hope that this series will help illuminate many of the complex issues involved in designing and implementing regulation and regulatory reforms at all levels of government.

ROBERT W. HAHN
ROBERT E. LITAN
AEI-Brookings Joint Center
for Regulatory Studies

1
Introduction

Industries with important network features have long been a concern of public policy in the United States. Indeed, railroads, one of the earliest industries to receive formal federal regulation through the creation of the Interstate Commerce Commission in 1887, are an archetypal network industry.[1] Those public policy concerns continue today, over 100 years later, not only for railroads but for many other industries with important network elements: telephone, broadcasting, cable television, electricity, water pipelines, sewage systems, oil pipelines, natural gas pipelines, road and highway systems, bus transport, truck transport, airlines, inland water transport, ocean shipping, postal service, package delivery systems, refuse pickup systems, airline computer reservation systems, bank automated teller machine systems, bank and nonbank credit card systems, bank debit card systems, bank check and payment clearance systems, local real estate broker multiple listing services, and the Internet.

The long-standing public policy concerns over network industries are not accidental, because those industries often embody two major and widely recognized forms of potential market failure: significant economies of scale—with the potential for monopoly—and externalities. Nevertheless, measures to address those concerns have often been misguided, with the result that we have inefficient and anticompetitive regulation and government ownership of network industries. The economic deregulation in the late 1970s and early 1980s of a number of network industries—air and surface transportation, natural gas pipelines, and telecommunications—was a welcome reversal of that policy, but much more remains to be done.

This volume clarifies the concept of a network and elucidates some of the important features of networks as a framework for describing some of the public policy dilemmas that often attach to network industries. I then review in broad terms the major public policy approaches that the United States has adopted toward network industries and conclude by setting out regulatory and antitrust policy lessons. Specifically, I evaluate the economic deregulatory experience of the 1970s and 1980s, the principles underlying the 1982 AT&T antitrust consent decree, the essential facilities doctrine, universal service requirements, regulatory innovations, the monopoly power of local utilities, the auctioning of the electromagnetic spectrum, and privatization of government-owned network facilities.

A Clarification

In recent years the term *network industry* has become an expansive, all-inclusive term that appears to embrace almost any composite good or service embodying complementary components; examples include computer hardware and software, video cassettes and cassette recorders, and compact disks and disk players. Indeed, scholars have applied the terms *metaphorical networks*[2] and *virtual networks*[3] to describe the broader usages. Although using the lens of a network may impart important lessons and insights for reexamining some of the structural and competitive issues that follow from complementarity,[4] I do not adopt that expansive approach. Instead, I focus on those industries with physical or electronic linkages that create networks so that I can concentrate on the major industries and issues that have dominated and will continue to dominate policymakers' attention both nationally and internationally.

2
Some Basic
Network Concepts

Before examining general public policy dilemmas, we should consider the basic concepts of networks, particularly their architecture and features.

The Architecture of Networks

Networks comprise links that connect nodes.[5] Figure 2-1 shows a simple star network that could represent a local telephone system. Calls between *A* and *B*—and *A* and *C, D* and *F,* and so forth—are routed through a central node or switch *S.* Such a structure economizes on the number and length of links necessary to provide all possible node-to-node transactions, but it requires that the central nodes have the capacity and the capability to handle all transactions among the nodes.

Figure 2-2 shows a second possible configuration of a local network: a circular or ring structure. Again, the design economizes on the number of links, and a central node is unnecessary. But some transactions will have to travel longer distances—for example, *A* to *E* via *B, C,* and *D*—than would have been true for the star network, although some adjacent transactions—for example, *A* to *B*—will involve shorter distances. In addition, the capacity of the links will have to be greater, because they often merely provide third-party transport.

Figure 2-3 shows a third way of configuring the local

Figure 2-1 A Simple Star Network

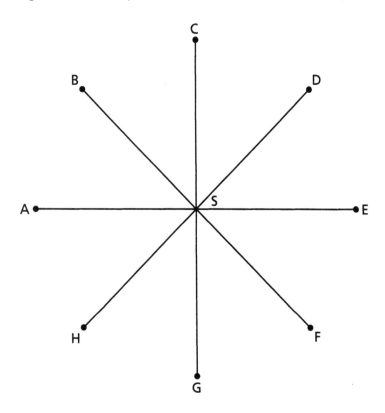

network: a structure in which all points are directly connected. That structure minimizes the direct distance for
completing a transaction between every pair of nodes, but
it requires the maximum number of links. It also, in principle, allows for alternative routings and thus has a back-
up capability, albeit through indirect routings. That
structure again eliminates the need for a central node, but
each node will require some capability for choosing among
links when a transaction is desired.

Figure 2-4 portrays two star networks and a trunk or
interface link $(S_A S_B)$ that connects their two central nodes

Figure 2-2   A Simple Ring Network

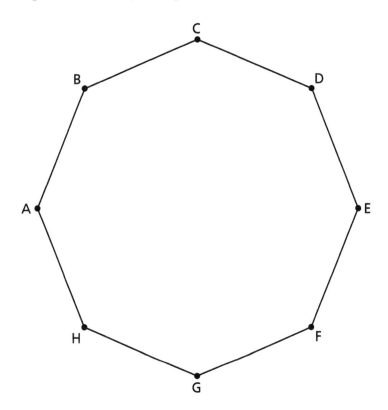

(S_A and S_B). We can interpret figure 2-4 as a simple representation of two local telephone systems connected by a long-distance link. With that configuration, the locally central nodes S_A and S_B provide local routing and switching and are also gateways and gathering points for long-distance transport.[6] That example readily demonstrates that connections among local or stand-alone networks create larger entities that are themselves networks.

The structure portrayed in figure 2-4 permits us easily to make an important distinction between two kinds of networks: two-way networks and one-way networks.[7] For two-

Figure 2-3　A Network with All Points Directly Connected

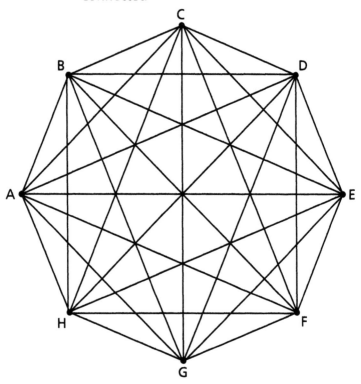

way networks, transactions can originate at any noncentral node and terminate at any noncentral node. Thus, if figure 2-4 or figures 2-1 through 2-3 portray a telephone system—or a rail, road, or airline system—a transaction (a call or a shipment) can originate at any A_i or B_j node and terminate at any other A_i or B_j node. The transaction $A_1 S_A A_2$ would be a local call or shipment; the transaction $A_3 S_A S_B B_1$ would be a long-distance call or shipment; and calls or shipments can flow in any direction.[8]

By contrast, in a one-way network some noncentral nodes are distinguished from others, and sensible trans-

Figure 2-4   Two Star Networks Connected by a
Trunk Link

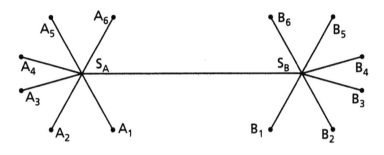

actions can flow in only one direction. Moreover, transactions between nodes of the same category also make no sense. For example, if figure 2-4 portrayed an electricity grid, the A nodes would represent electricity generation facilities, the link $S_A S_B$ would represent high-voltage bulk transmission wires,[9] S_B would be a local step-down and distribution station, and the B nodes would be individual users of electricity. Similarly, if figure 2-4 portrayed a cable television system, the A nodes would represent the various channels or networks that provide programming, $S_A S_B$ would be the links that collect the programming, send it up to a satellite, and return it to an earth station, S_B would be the local cable system's head-end facility, and the B nodes would be the subscribers to the local cable television service. In both examples, the flow of the relevant service—electricity or programming—occurs in only one direction—from the A nodes to the B nodes—and service flows between the A nodes or between the B nodes make no sense.[10]

We can categorize each of the various network industries into two-way or one-way classes. Two-way networks comprise telephone, roads and highways, bus transport, truck transport,[11] airlines, rail transport, inland water transport, ocean shipping, postal service, package delivery systems, bank check and payment clearance systems, multiple listing services, and Internet e-mail and chat groups. One-way networks comprise broadcasting, cable television, electricity, water pipelines,[12] sewage systems, oil pipelines, gas pipelines, refuse pickup systems, airline computer reservation systems, bank ATM systems,[13] bank debit card systems, credit card systems, and the Internet's World Wide Web. The distinction between one-way and two-way networks is important in understanding the type of externalities that may attach to a network.

Features of Networks

Common features of networks include externalities, economies of scale, compatibility, and standards.

Externalities. Consider, first, two-way networks. Suppose that a person joins a network that already has n nodes, for example, a telephone system, so that there are now $n + 1$ nodes. Then, in addition to the n potential types of transactions or calls that are open to the new member, he is now a potential recipient of calls from the incumbent n members. So long as the network has adequate capacity to accommodate the additional calls—so that the new person does not create significant congestion or interference costs for incumbent network members—or can add sufficient capacity at marginal costs that are less than or equal to the average capacity costs of serving the incumbent members, the new person will increase the value of the network to the incumbent members because they can now receive calls from and initiate calls to the new member.[14] That is a direct and genuine technological externality.[15]

Since the transaction flow occurs in only one direction in one-way networks, the reciprocal flow that creates the externality for two-way networks is absent. Instead, the externality occurs in a more indirect fashion, operating through unexploited economies of scale.[16] Here, we have two possibilities. The first involves just the straightforward existence of economies of scale. For example, suppose that a new person becomes a consumer on an electricity network. If unexploited economies of scale exist in generation or transmission,[17] then the new consumer reduces the costs of serving all the other members of the network. The second possibility involves economies of scale and the value of diversity. Suppose that a banks form an ATM network and that their estimate of the demand for ATM services causes them to offer only b ATM locations: because the operation of an ATM involves economies of scale, banks cannot justify a larger number of ATMs. If the demand for ATM services increases because more consumers move into the relevant geographic area, the banks may find it worthwhile to establish an additional location for an ATM, so that there are now $b + 1$ ATMs. The additional ATM location will increase the convenience to customers by reducing transportation and transactions costs for incumbent users.[18] Both kinds of economies of scale for one-way networks constitute genuine externalities, albeit of a more indirect nature than the externalities of two-way networks.[19]

Economies of Scale. Networks' links and central nodes often, although not always, exhibit significant economies of scale or scope[20] for some technologies and for low volumes of transactions. Indeed, the presence of unexploited economies of scale lies at the heart of the externalities for one-way networks, and either economies of scale or constant returns to scale can support the externalities of two-way networks.

It is important to note that significant economies of scale need not pervade all aspects of all links or nodes of all networks at all times. For some technologies, sufficiently large volumes of traffic may effectively exhaust the economies of scale, or the managerial difficulties of operating a sufficiently large firm may overwhelm any technologically driven economies. For those sufficiently large volumes, the marginal and average costs of providing service may be roughly constant with respect to volume or even increasing with volume. That exhaustion or overwhelming of economies of scale could be true for an entire network or just for parts of it. The volumes of traffic for air, rail, truck, bus, or telephone between New York City and Pittsburgh are likely to be much greater—at comparable prices and qualities—than between New York and Plattsburgh. It is quite possible that the economies of scale in serving the former city pair[21] could be exhausted at the larger volume,[22] while unexploited economies could still be available in serving the latter city pair. Also, separate from the density effects in each of the city pairs would be the question of whether the central node—New York—has economies or diseconomies of scale from the accumulation of traffic from all the city pairs that are linked directly to it and thus whether a single entity's ownership of multiple connected links creates economies or diseconomies of scope.

Compatibility. If a transaction within a network such as a call or a shipment is to be successful, the various nodes and links must be compatible with each other: they must use the same technology or similar enough technologies so that the costs of the transaction are not unduly increased.[23] Compatibility need not be an all-or-nothing phenomenon: close technologies may permit transactions to proceed with some impairment of quality, such as static on a telephone call, or of function because a pulse-dial telephone cannot perform so many functions as a tone-dial telephone, or at higher cost. In addition, a converter or translator device or technology may allow otherwise incompatible technologies to be fully or partially compatible, albeit at some increase in cost or decrease in quality.[24] Compatibility may involve not only formal technology such as electronics but also physical fitting such as a plug and a receptacle-jack or railroad track gauge and wheel-bogie spacings.

Standards. A way for the members of a network to achieve compatibility is to agree on a set of standards that would cover physical fitting as well as the formal technology. If a single entity owns the network, as did AT&T for telephones before 1984 and as did Citibank for ATMs before 1991, the entity achieves the standards and resulting compatibility by fiat. If multiple parties own parts of the network, then some forms of explicit agreement or implicit understanding, for example, through market imitation, will be necessary.

A good illustration of the compatibility and standards phenomenon—its costs, problems, efforts at translators, costs of achieving compatibility, and the benefits of compatibility—is the experience of the U.S. railroad system in the 1870s and 1880s, fifty years after the first development of railroads in the United States:

> The diversity of [track] gauge, especially in the South, ... made impossible the cross-country shipment of freight without break of bulk. . . .
>
> Standard automatic couplers and air brakes could do little to speed or facilitate freight traffic as long as a diversity of [track] gauge persisted. In 1861 more than 46 per cent of the nation's rail mileage was other than the 4 feet 8-1/2 inch standard gauge. . . .
>
> Several expedients were used in the sixties and seventies to permit the interchange of equipment between lines of different gauge. The "compromise car" was the simplest. Having wheels whose tread was five inches wide, the cars could be used on either standard-gauge track or track as wide as 4 feet 10 inches. However, careful railroad operators frowned upon the use of such cars because they claimed that many accidents could be traced to them. A second innovation, the car with wheels that could be made to slide along the axle, was no safer and was never widely adopted. Car hoists, or "elevating machines," with the cars lifted to a set

of trucks of different gauge, were much safer and were used extensively. . . . A number of lines also went to "double gauge," the addition of a third rail, permitting the use of equipment of different gauge.

There was no substitute for the adoption of a single gauge by the whole nation. In the early eighties most of the gauge divergence was found in the narrow-gauge lines of the mountain West and in the Old South, where the five-foot-gauge mileage had actually increased from 7,300 miles during the Civil War to more than 12,000 miles in 1880. The Chesapeake & Ohio, the Illinois Central, and the Mobile & Ohio had all changed to the narrower standard gauge by the middle eighties. James C. Clark, general manager of the Illinois Central lines south of Cairo, spent weeks of careful preparation for his change of gauge in the spring and early summer of 1881. On July 29, 1881, between dawn and 3:00 P.M., 3,000 workers shifted the gauge on the entire 550-mile line.

The rest of the South soon gave in. Representatives of southern lines totaling more than 13,000 miles agreed early in February 1886, to change their gauge the following May 31 and June 1. During the weeks before the day of the change, part of the southern rolling stock and motive power was changed to the narrower gauge and track gangs moved alternate inside spikes on one rail to the new position. . . . Using track gangs of from three to five men, ten roads west of the mountains shifted their rail on the last day of May. The remaining roads shifted June first. On both days the work was accomplished between 3:30 A.M. and 4:00 P.M., during which all traffic was stopped. Southern railroads had truly become part of the national network, and passenger or freight trains could move from any southern depot to any part of the nation without change of trucks or bulk. . . .

An immediate dividend of increased operating efficiency resulted from gauge standardization as a system of more extensive car interchange developed among the railroad companies.[25]

3

The General Public
Policy Dilemmas

The market imperfections related to networks' externalities, economies of scale, compatibility, and standards raise potential public policy concerns. We should, however, note that no industry fits perfectly the microeconomics textbook model of perfect competition; market imperfections occur in virtually any real-world industry. Although one might assume that those imperfections require widespread government intervention, the concept of the perfectly intervening government that only improves upon market imperfections is equally a textbook fiction; real-world governments too have their imperfections.[26] Accordingly, the presence of market imperfections does not automatically justify government intervention. In the end, the choice between unfettered markets and a continuum of potential government interventions should rest on empirical experience and observation—guided by theory—and cannot be settled by pure theory or ideology alone.

Externalities

With positive externalities, an individual's actions convey uncompensated benefits to others, outside a direct market contact.[27] In such circumstances, less than the socially appropriate—where social marginal benefits equal social marginal costs—level of the relevant activity occurs, and insufficient effort is devoted to enhancing the externality.[28] If a network has significant externalities, then that network will be smaller than is socially optimal. In principle, the incumbent members of the network could tax themselves to provide subsidies to encourage greater membership in the network and could still on net be better off.

Economies of Scale

If unexploited economies of scale characterize the production of a good or service, the most efficient arrangement is to consolidate production in a single firm. If that good or service is sufficiently distinct, however, the single producer will be a monopoly and will have market power: the ability to restrict output, distort quality, maintain prices that are above long-run marginal costs, and earn monopoly rents.[29] Since unexploited economies of scale appear to be a feature of some components of some networks, monopoly is a potential problem.

Monopoly need not be the only outcome for a network, however. If the economies of scale of the major components can be exhausted at commercially practicable volumes or if rival networks can differentiate themselves sufficiently, then multiple overlapping networks that compete over some or all of their links are a realistic possibility. Indeed, competing networks exist in railroads, trucking, airlines, long-distance telephone, local cellular telephone, airline computer reservation systems, credit card systems, broadcast networks, and even cable TV systems in a few local areas. Again, technology and volume effects may allow competition to occur over some links and at some nodes but not at others. In early 1999, for example, five airlines offered direct service between New York and Pittsburgh, while only one airline offered direct service between New York and Plattsburgh.[30]

Even if competition is present in most of the components of a network, monopoly in just a single component may be sufficient to capture all the potential rents from the transactions that use that component, since the linking components are often used in fixed proportions. Figure 2-4 can help illustrate that proposition. Suppose that the network in figure 2-4 represents a rail system or a telephone system. The link A_1S_A is a local rail siding or branch line or the twisted pair of copper wires that constitute the local loop; S_A is a marshaling yard or local switch; S_AS_B is a long-distance rail or telephone trunk line; S_B is a marshaling yard or local switch at the other end of the long-distance line; and S_BB_1 is the corresponding siding or local loop. For rail shipments or telephone calls between A_1 and B_1, monopoly ownership of any one of the components or links should be sufficient to capture any rents that are available from the transaction. If two or more monopolists own connecting links, however, their difficulties—or myopia— in bargaining over their claims to the monopoly rents may cause yet higher prices, lower output, and greater inefficiency, while also reducing the appropriated monopoly rents.[31] Unified ownership of the links—vertical integration—is a solution to that problem.[32]

If a monopoly owner of a single link can extract all the potential rents, then vertical integration—expanding ownership to adjacent links—ought not to interfere with the efficiency of the network transactions and could even improve efficiency if genuine economies of vertical integration exist or if a double-monopoly problem is thereby eliminated. Again, the presence of competition on adjacent links ought not to inhibit the ability of a monopolist of a single link to extract the appropriable rents. But if the adjacent links also serve other markets and significant economies of scale are present in those adjacent links, then vertical integration—combined with foreclosure or price squeezes vis-à-vis competitors on the vertical links—could enhance the monopolist's power and decrease network efficiency. For example, in figure 2-4 suppose that a firm has a monopoly over link A_1S_A and that competitors with somewhat differentiated products are present on trunk link

$S_A S_B$, with economies of scale also present on that latter link. By integrating into the latter link and then refusing to deal with its competitors on that link—or effecting a price squeeze—the monopolist may then be able to monopolize the latter link. Although his profits on the A_1-originating transactions will not increase, the monopolist will be able to extract rents on other transactions that use the $S_A S_B$ trunk link.[33] Similarly, if transactions costs[34] or regulation[35] constrain the monopolist of the original link from extracting all the potential rents, then again vertical integration combined with foreclosure or price squeezes may enhance his market power and decrease network efficiency.

An additional point concerns monopoly and network externalities. A common solution to the externality problem is to try to internalize the costs or benefits that are otherwise external to the party initiating the action. A single owner of a network might seem to be able to internalize the externalities and improve the network's efficiency as compared with the outcome from a group of competitors. If the single owner is a monopolist and cannot practice price discrimination, however, his incentive to restrict output is likely to outweigh any effect from internalization, and the monopoly outcome will be inferior—with lower output and higher prices—to a competitive outcome.[36]

Compatibility and Standards

As noted, a single owner establishes compatibility among the links and nodes of a network by fiat. With multiple actual or potential participants, however, problems may arise. Adopting one technology or standard over another may well favor some participants over others. The bargaining strengths of the participants, which may be related to their market shares, absolute sizes, and even pure bargaining skills, as well as the merits of the technologies themselves may determine outcomes.[37] To limit competition and enhance their market power, incumbent participants may agree on a technology that disadvantages potential entrants, maverick existing participants, or both.[38] An outcome that achieves the maximum technological and allocative (pricing) efficiency need not occur, unless the network is one among many competing networks and the competitive processes among the networks are sufficient to restrict the exercise of market power and weed out inefficient technologies.

Also, for some types of networks, when multiple new technologies arise—some of which are incompatible with existing equipment[39]—the potential obsolescence and nonfunctionality of existing stranded equipment in users' hands may create trade-offs between the higher quality that an incompatible technology offers and the lesser quality that technology compatible with the installed equipment base offers. The larger that installed base is, the more difficult that trade-off may be.[40]

Again, the example of the U.S. railroad system in the last half of the nineteenth century demonstrates the problems that arise when compatibility is an important feature of a network.

Pricing

If the network is a true monopoly, then the pricing of its services will reflect its market power: prices will be higher and outputs lower than if competitive principles, such as that price equals long-run marginal cost, were being followed. Even if multiple companies compete among themselves in providing a monopoly network's services, a joint venture among them—such as for owning and maintaining an indivisible component like a central switch or for ensuring compatibility in technology decisions—could be the vehicle for allowing them jointly to exercise market power. If entry to the network is restricted, the joint venture could levy fees on its members' transactions that would capture the monopoly rents of the network and then return the proceeds to its members according to a non-volume-sensitive formula so as to prevent the competing away of the rents.[41] On a related point, serious questions exist as to how much control such a joint venture should be permitted to exercise over the pricing and other behavior of its members. Although the joint venture could have legitimate efficiency-enhancing reasons for restricting its members' behavior,[42] those restrictions could also be a vehicle for the members' joint exercise of market power.[43] Again, of course, such concerns are of much less import if the network in question is just one among many in a relevant market and the network has little or no market power to exercise unilaterally.

As we noted, if a firm has monopoly power with respect to one or more components of a network but competes with other firms with respect to other components, the firm's monopoly position may not be sufficient to allow it to gain all appropriable rents. Consequently, the monopolist may have an incentive to foreclose or refuse to deal with his actual or potential rivals in the complementary components. Equivalently and less blatantly, the monopolist may try to perform a price squeeze vis-à-vis his rivals in the complementary components. In essence, the monopolist would overcharge his rivals for using his monopoly component in providing through service.

One prominent suggestion for judging the allocative efficiency of a monopolist's pricing of his services to rivals with complementary components is the efficient component pricing rule.[44] That rule states that a monopolist should be allowed to charge a price that covers his opportunity costs, including forgone net revenues in his sale of the complementary component. Although the application of the rule would encourage technological efficiency by ensuring that only more efficient rivals than the monopolist could produce the complementary component and hence the "through" service, the rule would also preclude the price-reducing competitive challenges that even less efficient rivals could generate.[45]

The Imperfections of Public Policy

We have considered many potential problems that attach to network industries. In principle, omniscient government agencies' wise and careful application of public policy should correct those problems. The proper definition and enforcement of property rights or an appropriate set of taxes and subsidies can cure externality problems. A set of taxes and subsidies or a regulatory edict that requires that prices be equal to long-run marginal costs can solve monopoly problems.[46] A wise government would ensure that a network would choose only appropriate technologies.

In practice, governments are not omniscient. They are almost always at an informational disadvantage compared with the parties that they are trying to influence—partly because of inherent principal-agent problems[47] and partly because of the mixed or cloudy incentive structure that typically applies to government agencies.[48] Thus, in undertaking even the simple task of limiting a monopoly to a competitive rate of return, a government regulatory agency is always at a severe disadvantage with respect to the regulated entity in trying to determine the latter's efficient cost levels as well as in determining crucial demand parameters and the appropriate level of profits. If the regulatory agency allows a profit level that is excessive, not only will the monopoly set inappropriately high prices, but it will also waste resources by investing in excessive amounts of capital equipment and choosing excessively capital-intensive technologies and offering more capital-intensive products and services;[49] if the regulatory agency constrains the profit level at an insufficient level, prices will be excessively low, and the monopolist will attempt to skimp on quality.[50] The regulator will find it difficult to determine whether the firm is operating efficiently at any given point in time and whether it is efficiently embracing technological improvements as they are available. Indeed, if the regulator is successful at keeping the monopolist's profits at just competitive levels, the monopolist will have little or no incentive to embrace new technologies, since he could not thereby gain extra profits.

Further, governments may not be the benevolent neutral entities of textbooks. The parties affected by governmental decisions are likely to expend resources to influence those decisions. The larger and more concentrated are the consequences of a governmental decision, the greater are the incentives for a party to lobby or otherwise try to influence the outcome.[51] Thus, involving a governmental body in determining a network's technology standard may simply shift the focus of the bargaining and negotiation toward government, with no assurance of a superior outcome. With respect to monopoly regulation, customers may not be satisfied with an overall limitation on profits but may lobby for specific levels or patterns of prices. If those prices require cross-subsidy, then new firms may be tempted to enter and cream skim by offering lower-priced service to customers to whom monopolies charge prices above long-run marginal cost. Alternatively, changes in technology may reduce the crucial levels of economies of scale and permit entry, which is most likely to occur in the most profitable areas. But the regulated entity would be likely to resist entry in any event—especially when it occurs in its most profitable areas—and the parties that are favored by cross-subsidy are likely also to oppose entry. The pressures on the regulatory agency to restrict entry may well be formidable.

On a different tack, the firms in an industry may simply conclude that competition is unpleasant and collectively lobby to gain regulatory protection—from their own competitive efforts and from those of potential entrants.

In sum, the efforts of government to fix the potential problems of networks may well go awry. A consciousness of that possibility should inform—though not automatically condemn—all suggestions for regulatory initiatives.

4

A Broad Overview and Critique of Public Policy

To describe and critique the broad patterns of U.S. public policy toward network industries, we can usefully classify its expanse into three major areas: regulation, antitrust, and government ownership.[52]

Regulation

Formal regulation at the federal, state, and local levels has at various times affected many network industries: railroads, trucking, airlines, bus lines, gas pipelines, oil pipelines, electricity, telephone, cable television, water systems, and refuse pickup systems. Regulation usually aims to limit the exercise of monopoly power, primarily by capping the level of profit that the firm can earn. Achieving that goal while ensuring that the firm operates efficiently is extremely difficult even under the best of circumstances.

Another important regulatory goal is to prevent firms from unduly discriminating in the prices they charge to various classes of customers—maintaining fairness in pricing. Such goals have often led to implicit or explicit systems of cross-subsidy, including must-serve requirements on unprofitable services or routes, since popular notions of fairness often focus on comparisons of prices and neglect comparative costs.[53] The cross-subsidy has often favored households at the expense of businesses, rural residents at the expense of urban residents, and raw material shipments at the expense of manufactured goods.[54] Then, to maintain and preserve such a system, regulators have had to prevent entry and restrict competition generally, especially price competition.[55] Sometimes policymakers have justified restraining that competition by asserting that they were restraining "excessive" competition.[56] Nationality-ownership restrictions on who could provide domestic service have also protected some industries from foreign competition.[57]

As critics of U.S. regulation complained in the 1960s and 1970s[58] and as the deregulation of the 1980s and 1990s subsequently demonstrated,[59] both customers and firms paid a substantial cost in terms of the inefficiency of the regulatory outcomes—especially the restrictions on competition. Particularly egregious were the imposition in the 1930s of rate and must-serve regulation on interstate trucking and airlines, which were and continue to be fundamentally not monopolistic,[60] and the inhibitions on burgeoning competition in pieces of the telephone system from the early 1960s until the early 1980s. Further, regulation directly and indirectly delayed and discouraged technological improvements in processes and products.[61]

In addition, cost levels in those industries tended to be higher because their labor forces were highly unionized and their unions were aggressive in seeking relatively high wage levels and costly work rules. The link between unionization, network industries, and regulation was not accidental. Many of the regulated network firms were relatively large, which reduced the per-person costs of organizing. With regulatory inhibitions on competition and entry, the population of firms was relatively stable; once the labor force of an industry was organized, it stayed organized. In addition, union leaders did not have to worry about entry and competition from nonunion firms. Indeed, labor unions were among the fiercest opponents of deregulation. Tellingly, a significant amount of the gains from deregulation have come from reductions in labor costs.[62]

We should not, however, view that regulatory pattern as one of regulators' running amok and ignoring the will of the people. Elected legislators, after all, had enacted the enabling pieces of legislation; elected presidents and governors had signed them. Legislatures had held numerous review and assessment hearings and had periodically crafted modest modifications and refinements. The American polity seemed content with such arrangements.[63]

A fundamental change began in the late 1970s.[64] Within less than a decade, the federal government deregulated air, rail, truck, and bus transport and natural gas production and transport with respect to rates, entry, and exit,[65] and, with some lag and reluctance, the states largely followed. In addition, spurred by the Justice Department's successful conclusion—via a 1982 consent decree—to its antitrust suit against AT&T that vertically disintegrated the telephone network and separated the largely competitive long-distance services and equipment manufacturing from the local monopoly services, the Federal Communications Commission became much more competitively inclined; the states, unfortunately, have been much slower to follow.[66]

The deregulatory movement has generally decreased costs and prices substantially, improved service quality, and substantially increased efficiency and social welfare.[67] Further, in some regulatory jurisdictions and for some telephone services, regulators have moved away from profit-based, rate-of-return regulation of monopoly services with its potential for creating inefficiencies and have substituted partial forms of price-cap regulation with price ceilings linked to general rates of inflation and estimates of likely productivity improvements in the telephone industry. Price-cap regulation has both positive and negative features. It creates a stronger incentive for the regulated firm to operate efficiently—to innovate and reduce costs—since it need not fear that the regulator will immediately remove any gain by forcing a commensurate decrease in prices; and the regulator need not try to determine the firm's efficient level of costs, including the appropriate rate of profit on the appropriate capital base and excluding all costs that are unnecessary. On the minus side, misspecifying the price index and the productivity improvement index could lead to either wholly inadequate profits or wildly excessive profits, with either condition's causing regulators to respecify the price-cap formula and thus undermine the basic notion that price-cap regulation is supposed to provide an unalloyed incentive for the firm to behave efficiently.[68] Despite those drawbacks, the change to price-cap regulation is likely to improve efficiency.[69]

Two additional changes in regulation occurred. First, a combination of federal and local regulation affected the cable television industry from the birth of the industry in the 1950s through the 1970s. To protect local over-the-air television broadcasters, the FCC restricted the programming that cable systems could offer, and municipalities limited the prices that the systems could charge; municipalities also exacted franchise fees and in-kind services such as dedicated access channels. In the late 1970s, however, the FCC reduced its restrictions on programming, and in 1984 Congress, reacting to the cable operators' complaints of onerous local regulation, largely freed cable television from local regulation.[70] In the early 1990s, however, Congress, reacting to subscribers' complaints of excessive rates, imposed federal rate regulation. The Telecommunications Act of 1996 promised yet another reversal by largely freeing cable rates from regulation by the late 1990s.[71]

Second, with respect to the use of the electromagnetic spectrum by network industries, the FCC throughout almost all of its existence has allocated spectrum to various uses and users. Efficiency of use has often not been a high priority. In the early 1990s, however, Congress—responding more to the potential revenue-raising attributes of auctions than to their allocative efficiency—authorized the FCC to auction limited parts of the spectrum. Although that is a welcome beginning, we have yet to see the full consequences of those auctions, and the commission should extend its use of pricing mechanisms in allocating spectrum.

Of the regulatory commissions, the FCC has been one of the most seriously involved in setting standards and maintaining compatibility for the network industries that it regulates.[72] It has, however, refrained from imposing standards for some technologies. In at least one instance (TV stereo), the industry was nevertheless able to coalesce on a standard. For AM radio stereo, however, a set of competing standards and technologies briefly appeared in the marketplace, but no standard achieved widespread acceptance, and AM stereo has faded from the marketplace.

Where the stakes were high—basic television standards in the early 1940s, color television standards in the early 1950s, high-definition television standards in the late 1980s and early 1990s—the FCC took an active role in setting standards, and the commission appears to have largely succeeded in generating industry consensuses and in avoiding large mistakes, with the exception of its initial blunder with color television.[73]

Antitrust

U.S. antitrust policy has affected both regulated and unregulated network industries. An important antitrust concern is whether network owners have refused to provide access to rivals or have treated them in a discriminatory fashion. That was the basic notion underlying the Justice Department's pursuit of vertical divestiture in its AT&T antitrust case and also underlying a set of legal decisions involving what the courts have called essential facilities.

The AT&T Case. The Justice Department's view of the AT&T problem was straightforward.[74] It saw long-distance telephone service and equipment manufacturing as fundamentally not monopolistic industries, while local telephone service was a bottleneck monopoly. So long as AT&T

possessed the monopoly in local service, it could discriminate against its rivals in long-distance service and manufacturing and effectively deny or distort their access to AT&T's
local networks.[75] The solution was to divest local service
operations from AT&T's other activities.[76] The government
achieved that outcome with a 1982 Modification of Final
Judgment that effected divestiture on January 1, 1984.[77]

Although one can quibble with the impact of antitrust
and regulatory policy on telephone networks since 1984,
the basic concept underlying the Justice Department's case
was—and is—sound and is a useful precedent for policy in
other network industries where some pieces are actually or
potentially competitive and other pieces are monopolistic.

The Essential Facilities Doctrine. Beginning at least in 1912,
antitrust court decisions addressed the access of competitors to essential facilities, a concern that has come to be
known as the "essential facilities doctrine."[78] Courts have
explicitly applied that doctrine to a railroad,[79] a collectively
owned railroad terminal,[80] the telephone system,[81] and local real estate multiple listing services.[82] Courts have used
that doctrine as the implicit basis for decisions applying to
a news service,[83] an electricity system,[84] and a skiing facility.[85] Indeed, the essential facilities doctrine underlies the
common law notions of common carrier obligations. Further, during the 1980s the Department of Transportation
treated airline computer reservation systems as essential
facilities in antitrust-like regulatory proceedings that it
conducted.[86] The concern of the DOT and of the Justice
Department, which filed extensive comments in the pro-
ceeding, was that "host" airlines might use their ownership
of such systems to discriminate against and disadvantage
rivals—especially smaller or maverick airlines. DOT's final
decision enunciated a set of rules that were expected to
minimize discrimination.

Unfortunately, neither the courts nor Congress has
ever clearly specified what constitutes an essential facility

for antitrust purposes. Is it synonymous with monopoly or is it a narrower subset of monopoly? One has little guidance. Clearly, however, just the presence of a network does not automatically elevate that network to an essential facility.[87]

In addition to the overt essential facilities cases, the courts have addressed situations in which firms used the standard-setting processes of trade associations to disadvantage their rivals.[88] Neither of the two Supreme Court cases involved network industries, however.

Although antitrust activity with respect to networks has not been nearly so extensive as has formal regulation, antitrust's presence has been felt—especially in the AT&T case. As formal regulation of network industries diminishes, antitrust is likely to grow in importance. If it does, the courts, Congress, or both must clarify the essential facilities doctrine.

Government Ownership

Although government ownership of network industries is not so extensive in the United States as it is in most other countries, government ownership at the federal, state, or local level nevertheless plays a nontrivial role in networks. Network industries that government owns include: the postal system; television and radio networks; electric power;[89] water distribution systems; road and highway design, construction, and maintenance; sewage systems; refuse pickup systems; the air traffic control system; river, canal, and coastal port maintenance; national passenger rail transport; ferry systems; local bus and streetcar systems; and commuter bus and rail systems.[90]

The problems associated with regulation also plague government network enterprises: incentive problems in maintaining efficiency, unionized labor forces with high labor costs, pricing problems, and cross-subsidy. Also, to protect cross-subsidy efforts, regulation hobbles or prohibits such competitive alternatives as private delivery of first-class mail[91] and jitney operators in local transportation markets. In addition, with governmental tax revenues ultimately backing them, some of those networks' services—irrigation water is a prime example—are provided at prices far below long-run marginal costs. Also, for networks like roads, neither direct charges such as tolls nor indirect charges such as gasoline taxes—a rough-and-ready user fee—have followed marginal cost principles. Government owners rarely adopt peak-load pricing or congestion-sensitive fees, nor do they impose fees and taxes on heavy trucks that are proportionate to their wear and tear on the roads.

Despite the deregulation movement of the 1970s and 1980s, there have been no comparable movements toward privatizing government-owned network industries. The only notable exception was the privatization of Conrail in the 1980s.[92]

5
Policy Lessons and Conclusion

Public policy has played an extensive role in shaping the structure, behavior, and performance of network industries in the United States. Given the inherent characteristics of those industries, much of that involvement was probably inevitable.

The overall record of public policy is, at best, mixed. The AT&T divestiture stands out as a triumph of sound antitrust policy, and it is probable that local regulation of electric, natural gas, telephone, and water utilities has prevented the most serious monopoly abuses. It would likely not be a pleasant experience to be exposed to the unfettered pricing power of those firms, since the estimated price elasticities of demand for their basic services are typically quite low—well below –1.0.[93] Further, the federal deregulation of air and surface transportation has been an important public policy success—although its success lies primarily in undoing the regulatory morass that preceded it. On the other hand, the American economy has experienced and continues to experience substantial efficiency losses from the ill-conceived and ill-executed restrictions on competition and misguided pricing that characterize the regulatory regimes or government operation of many network industries.

The Lessons

We can draw a number of important lessons for public policy from this review. First, the economic deregulation of air and surface transportation, natural gas pipelines, and telecommunications in the late 1970s and early 1980s was an outstanding undertaking, albeit one that was largely undoing the damage of the previous five to eight decades. Policymakers should resist all calls to reregulate those industries. Further, policymakers should apply those economic deregulatory concepts to other network industries, along the lines suggested below.

Second, the basic principles underlying the AT&T divestiture—that a bottleneck monopoly should be under separate ownership from that of complementary competitive goods and services—has important applicability to other network industries that present mixtures of competitive and monopoly components. Natural gas pipelines and electricity grids are obvious examples; others are surely possible. Those two industries have their special historical legacies and problems: high-price energy contracts in the former industry and high-cost nuclear facilities in the latter. But the benefits from greater competition and wider customer choice are likely to be great. The natural gas industry has already substantially solved its problems; the electricity industry is just starting down the road.[94] Policymakers need to find ways to solve electricity's special problems.

Third, the courts, Congress, or both must clarify the essential facilities doctrine of antitrust. Doing so will be worthwhile solely to provide greater certainty to business enterprises and joint venturers. But as policymakers reduce the regulatory oversight of network industries and instead subject them to the checks and bounds of antitrust litigation brought by government prosecutors and private litigants, it will be even more imperative that firms have a clear sense of the essential facilities doctrine. An important guiding principle for any clarification must be the reaffirmation of the notion—sometimes enunciated in antitrust legal opinions[95] but sometimes also ignored in the actual decisions—that the purpose of antitrust is to support competition as a process and not to protect individual enterprises. That principle must mean that a network facing effective competition—so that its actions do not significantly affect marketplace outcomes—ought to enjoy more antitrust freedoms, for example, with respect to the complaints of a disgruntled customer or supplier or an excluded rival, than does the true bottleneck monopoly. That principle and its application are valid regardless of whether the network is a joint venture, such as a credit card or ATM network, or is a singly owned venture, such as a local telephone network.

Fourth, obligating a network to provide universal service is almost always antithetical to efficient pricing and ultimately to competition;[96] the same principle applies to must-serve obligations. That requirement inevitably means that some prices are not even sufficient to cover marginal costs and thus necessitates cross-subsidies. But cross-subsidization is not viable in a competitive world, because competition (from entrants as well as incumbent competitors) will surely "skim the cream" of high-profit areas that are supposed to provide the surplus to cover the below-cost offerings and thus causes prices to decline and the surplus to disappear. Hence, regulatory restrictions on entry and competition naturally follow in the wake of universal service and must-serve requirements. If having universal service serves a substantial public purpose, policymakers should achieve that outcome through the public fisc—not through the implicit processes of cross-subsidy and the regulatory inefficiencies that accompany it.

Fifth, regulation of true local monopolies is probably inevitable and warranted—again because the price elasticities of demand are so low. But policymakers should encourage regulatory innovations such as price caps to reduce the distorted incentives that regulation can easily generate. In addition, public policy advocates must be vigilant and vociferous in opposing the competitive restrictions and pricing distortions that have characterized much of regulation in the past and that still pervade local telephone regulation.

Sixth, the hope that entry will somehow sufficiently erode the monopoly power of local utilities, so that local regulation can be eliminated in the not-too-distant future, is probably misplaced, especially for facilities-based providers with substantial capital costs of local connections; the problem is yet more severe for two-way networks such as telephone systems.[97] Figure 2-1 provides a useful illustration. Suppose that in place of the monopoly central switch, a competing central switch were added. So long as all network users did not subscribe to both switches, links between the two switches would be necessary, so that subscribers to one switch could reach the subscribers to the other switch. And each switch owner would still be a monopolist with respect to the incoming calls from the other switch.[98]

There may, though, be two possible long-run solutions to the local monopoly problem in telephones. One solution would require that much or all local telephone service be spectrum-based.[99] If callers could readily use over-the-air transmissions—as opposed to copper wire—to reach and be reached by alternative switching facilities, the monopoly of the local switch would be eliminated. An alternative solution would require massive amounts of local fiber-optic cable—perhaps publicly provided and maintained—so that all telephone calls could go through all lines to all locations, where on-site identifiers would pull out only those calls intended for that location.[100] In essence, both solutions would create strong parallels to the competitive forces that trucks and public roads brought to surface transportation.[101]

Seventh, the FCC must continue and expand spectrum auctions and other pricing reforms to improve spectrum allocation.

Eighth, government ownership of network facilities should always be subject to frequent scrutiny and evaluation of the possibilities of privatization. At a minimum, the opening of government monopolies to the fresh breezes of competition is mandatory. A good place to start would be the legislative repeal of the Private Express Statutes, which prevent competition to the U.S. Postal Service in the delivery of first-class mail.[102] Similarly, policymakers should abolish the regulatory inhibitions on jitney and other formal and informal forms of transportation competition to government-operated local transportation systems. Again, pleas for the maintenance of universal service ought not to stand in the way of greater competition and the improved pricing and production efficiency that would accompany it—in postal service, local transportation, and virtually all other government-provided services as well.

Where the network is a true natural monopoly, the choice between government ownership and private ownership with regulatory oversight is not an easy one. Either arrangement has obvious efficiency drawbacks. Private production is, however, almost always more efficient than government production, and private enterprises are usually more receptive to technological change.[103] Those tendencies create a presumption toward privatization, especially where reformed regulation can keep potential excesses—public as well as private—in check.

For those cases in which government ownership remains, improved pricing policies such as peak-load pricing, congestion-sensitive pricing, and user-cost-sensitive pricing are vital for improving allocative efficiency.

Despite the substantial reforms of the past two decades, policymakers have much to do to improve the economic efficiency and competitiveness of network industries. One can only hope that the deregulatory momentum of those decades will carry forward through the next two.

Notes

1. Federal regulation of commercial banks—an industry with some network characteristics—extends even further back, beginning in 1863; and state regulation of banks began in the early nineteenth century. Further, federal and state interest and involvement in canals and turnpikes—network industries—also began in the early nineteenth century.

2. See Liebowitz and Margolis (1994).

3. See Katz and Shapiro (1994).

4. See Economides (1996).

5. Ibid.

6. Although we have shown the long-distance link connecting only two star networks, it is clearly possible for long-distance links to connect rings or networks with all points directly connected as well.

7. See Economides and White (1994).

8. In essence all the links and the central node are complements to each other; completed transactions, for example, calls or shipments, may be substitutes.

9. For an electricity grid, central node S_A may not exist, or it may be a gathering and coordinating station.

10. Again, the A links and central node are complements to the B links and central node; but the A links will be substitutes among themselves, as will be the B links. Almost all the metaphorical or virtual networks discussed by Katz and Shapiro (1994), Besen and Farrell (1994), and Liebowitz and Margolis (1994) are one-way networks. For another survey, see David and Greenstein (1990).

11. To the extent that some locations are primarily shippers rather than receivers and others, such as local supermarkets, are primarily receivers, a truck transport system might begin to look

35

more like a one-way network; still, in principle, all nodes can be connected to ship to all other nodes—the crucial aspect of two-way systems.

12. In theory, a water or other pipeline system might be reversible and hence two-way. In reality, the architecture of the pipes and the direction of the pumps—and of gravity—make it extremely unlikely that households would ever use the water system to pump water back to reservoirs or to each other.

13. ATMs can be used for deposits as well as for obtaining cash. In that sense, the flows can go two ways. Still, flows between ATMs do not occur, so classifying them as one-way networks seems best.

14. See Artle and Averous (1973) and Rohlfs (1974).

15. Even Liebowitz and Margolis (1994), who express the most skepticism about network externalities, grudgingly acknowledge the validity of that version of network externalities in principle, although they are even more skeptical as to its empirical or policy relevance.

16. Farrell and Saloner (1985) describe that as a "market-mediated effect."

17. But the managerial difficulties of operating a larger company might offset those technological economies. See Chamberlin (1956, appendix B).

18. Similarly, more subscribers to a cable TV system could justify more programming. Note that when the network externality causes one extra ATM to be added to the market, the number of *new* services is equal to a: the number of banks that can be combined with the new ATM. If the added demand were instead to allow a new bank to come into existence, the number of new services is b. By contrast, in a two-way network, when an extra node is added to a system of n nodes, $2n$ new transactions are possible.

19. Liebowitz and Margolis (1994) seem reluctant to acknowledge that network effects driven by economies of scale constitute a genuine externality. But the principle is valid: a tax-and-subsidy combination at the margin could be Pareto-improving.

20. As compared with the strict notion of economies of scale—the concept of unit costs' being lower when production volumes are higher for a narrowly defined good or service—economies of scope embody the notion that the aggregate costs of producing multiple products within a single ownership unit are lower than

the aggregate costs of producing the same volumes of the products within separate ownership units. For similar but not identical goods or services, the terms *economies of scale* and *economies of scope* are sometimes used interchangeably.

21. In a network context, those are often called economies of density.

22. Again, that could be due to the "natural" exhaustion of the technological economies of scale or to the progressive difficulties of managing a larger organization.

23. In many ways those issues of compatibility are basically ones of complementarity in a nonnetwork context. See Economides and White (1994).

24. For example, although European and U.S. television systems are incompatible, the two systems are now readily able to send and receive each other's transmissions.

25. Stover (1961, 149–56).

26. See Wolf (1989) and White (1994).

27. If the effects occur within a market, then the externalities are likely to be "pecuniary" rather than technological, and Pareto-improving actions are not available. See Liebowitz and Margolis (1994).

28. That is the mirror image of the negative externality, where the price is overly high, output is excessive, and insufficient effort is devoted to reducing the externality. At the heart of most externality problems are ill-defined or poorly enforced property rights. See Coase (1960).

29. The monopolist is limited in his ability to extract rents, of course, by demanders' willingness to pay, which is related to their incomes and the availability of close and distant substitutes.

30. See Port Authority of New York and New Jersey (1999).

31. That is often known as the problem of double marginalization. As Economides (1996) points out, Cournot (1927) was the first to recognize that problem in 1838.

32. Again, Cournot (1927) was the first to recognize that solution in 1838.

33. See Economides and White (1994) and Burton and Wilson (1995).

34. See Winston et al. (1990) and Grimm, Winston, and Evans (1992).

35. See Brennan (1987, 1990, 1995).

36. See Economides and Himmelberg (1995).

37. See Katz and Shapiro (1986, 1994), Farrell and Saloner (1985, 1986), and Besen and Farrell (1994).

38. Of course, a monopoly also may want to skew technology to favor itself vis-à-vis potential entrants or vis-à-vis rivals in complementary links.

39. Such was the case when color television was first developed in the United States in the late 1940s.

40. On the other hand, unregulated markets are capable of making those kinds of transitions. Over a period of about a decade, compact disks and players completely superseded phonograph records and players.

41. See Lewis and Reynolds (1979).

42. For example, in an ATM network, different prices for the same ATM services at different machines might confuse and anger customers and decrease the volume and value of the entire ATM network.

43. For a wide-ranging discussion, see Guerin-Calvert and Wildman (1991).

44. See Baumol and Sidak (1994a, 1994b).

45. See Economides and White (1995, 1998). See also Hausman and Tardiff (1995).

46. Of course, where common costs are not covered by prices equal to long-run marginal costs, some form of Ramsey pricing will be necessary to minimize allocative inefficiency. See Baumol and Bradford (1970).

47. See Baron (1989).

48. See Wolf (1989) and White (1994).

49. That is the so-called Averch-Johnson (1962) effect. For a discussion, see Baumol and Klevorick (1970).

50. See MacAvoy (1983).

51. See Stigler (1971), Posner (1971, 1974), Krueger (1974), Peltzman (1976), and Noll (1989).

52. Other reviews of public policy appear in Joskow and Rose (1989), Winston (1993), Joskow and Noll (1994), and White (1993c).

53. The Community Reinvestment Act of 1977 imposed cross-subsidy and must-serve requirements on the banking sector. See White (1993b).

54. With respect to the telephone network, a frequent justification for cross-subsidy is the claimed social benefit from univer-

sal service. Perhaps that is a nontechnical way of describing network externalities, but maybe not.

55. But rivalrous firms have often turned to nonprice competition. See White (1972, 1975).

56. Policymakers used the same justification to place the Regulation Q restraints on the interest rates that banks and thrift institutions could pay to their depositors.

57. Those restrictions still apply to airlines, telephone companies, broadcasters, and coastal shipping.

58. See, for example, Meyer et al. (1959), Caves (1962), and Friedlaender (1969).

59. See Winston (1993); see also Moore (1986), Morrison and Winston (1986), MacDonald (1989), Burton (1995), Wilson (1994), and Teske, Best, and Mintrom (1995).

60. See Meyer et al. (1959), Caves (1962), Friedlaender (1969), Friedlaender and Spady (1981), and Morrison and Winston (1986).

61. In rail the introductions of unit trains and "Big John" cars were delayed by the Interstate Commerce Commission's concerns that the reduced costs of those innovations might give innovators an "unfair" advantage over their rivals; see MacAvoy and Sloss (1967). In air transport the discovery and development of the hub-and-spokes system for flight scheduling had to await the demise of the Civil Aeronautics Board's mandatory and ubiquitous route assignments. And AT&T's pre-1982 discouragement of non-AT&T attachments and connections to its network and equipment surely delayed and discouraged innovative combinations and arrangements. But some critics have argued that the post-1984 divestiture arrangements have also delayed and discouraged innovation. See MacAvoy (1996).

62. See McFarland (1989), Winston (1993), and Wilson (1994).

63. See Stigler (1971), Posner (1971, 1974), Krueger (1974), Peltzman (1976), and Noll (1989).

64. In reality, the U.S. Department of Justice led the way in the late 1960s and early 1970s by pressuring the New York Stock Exchange and the Securities and Exchange Commission to end the price-fixing arrangements that had previously prevailed with respect to stock brokerage commissions.

65. Also, petroleum price regulation—a vestige from the Nixon price controls of the early 1970s—was removed in 1981, and banks and thrifts experienced substantial deregulation. Unfortunately,

unlike airlines and trucking, where safety regulation remained largely intact, the thrift industry additionally experienced a reduction in safety regulation in the early 1980s—with disastrous eventual consequences. See White (1991, 1993a).

66. A glaring example has been the states' reluctance to permit competition in short-distance toll services, so as to preserve a cross-subsidy from those services to basic local service.

67. See Winston (1993).

68. In essence, the latter problem means that, in practice, price-cap regulation will be somewhat similar to rate-of-return regulation with a lag.

69. For further discussion of price-cap regulation, comparisons with rate-of-return regulation, and potential problems, see Braeutigam (1989), Sappington and Sibley (1992), Laffont and Tirole (1993), Weisman (1993, 1994), and Sappington and Weisman (1996).

70. See Owen and Gottlieb (1986).

71. See Hazlett and Spitzer (1997).

72. See, for example, Besen and Johnson (1986).

73. The FCC in 1950 approved a color system that was not compatible with existing black-and-white sets. The system was not commercially successful, and in 1953 the FCC ratified a different system that was compatible with existing black-and-white sets. See Besen and Johnson (1986, chap. 7).

74. See Evans (1983), Brennan (1987, 1990, 1995), Crandall (1991), Brock (1994), and Noll and Owen (1994).

75. AT&T's presence in long-distance and manufacturing also gave it the opportunity to misallocate costs away from those competitive areas and into the regulated local service area so that it could earn higher profits in the latter area and possibly even expand its output in the former area. That expansion could occur if the misallocated costs were marginal, thus lowering the effective marginal costs that would serve as the basis for pricing in those competitive areas.

76. The department assumed that there were few or no significant economies of vertical integration that would thereby be sacrificed.

77. The Telecommunications Act of 1996 supersedes the 1982 Modification of Final Judgment and permits the regional Bell operating companies, subject to certain conditions set out in a

competitive checklist, to enter long-distance markets. See MacAvoy (1996) and Vogelsang and Mitchell (1997).

78. See Werden (1988), Ratner (1988), and Reiffen and Kleit (1990).

79. See *Delaware & Hudson Railway Co.* v. *Consolidated Rail Corp.*, 902 F.2d 174 (1990).

80. See *United States* v. *Terminal Railroad Association of St. Louis*, 224 U.S. 383 (1912).

81. See *MCI Communications* v. *American Tel. & Tel. Co.*, 708 F.2d 1081 (1983).

82. See Lopatka and Simons (1991) and the cases cited there.

83. See *Associated Press* v. *United States*, 326 U.S. 1 (1945).

84. See *Otter Tail Power Co.* v. *United States*, 410 U.S. 366 (1973).

85. See *Aspen Skiing Co.* v. *Aspen Highland Skiing Corp.*, 472 U.S. 585 (1985).

86. See Guerin-Calvert (1994).

87. That was made evident in a recent case in which the VISA credit card network denied membership to a Utah thrift institution that was owned at the time by Sears, which also owned and operated the Discover Card network; the thrift's subsequent antitrust suit did not succeed in the courts. See *SCFC ILC, Inc.* v. *VISA USA, Inc.*, 36 F.2d 958 (1994). For a discussion of that case, see Carlton and Frankel (1995a, 1995b), Evans and Schmalensee (1995, 1999), and Carlton and Salop (1996).

88. See *Radiant Burners, Inc.* v. *Peoples Gas Light & Coke Co.*, 364 U.S. 656 (1961), and *American Society of Mechanical Engineers, Inc.* v. *Hydrolevel Corp.*, 456 U.S. 556 (1982).

89. Examples include the Tennessee Valley Authority, the Columbia River Power Authority, the New York Power Authority, and the Los Angeles Department of Water and Power.

90. Also, the United States briefly nationalized its entire railroad system during World War I, and the federal government operated the Conrail freight system for a decade and a half—from the early 1970s until the mid-1980s. Alaska operates a railroad system.

91. See Sidak and Spulber (1996).

92. Although the privatization of Amtrak is a perennial topic for discussion and fulmination in Congress, the actual actions taken have involved only reductions in the level of federal subsidy and the consequent contractions in Amtrak's route structure and departure frequencies.

93. For basic telephone, see Taylor (1994); for electricity, see Joskow and Schmalensee (1983). The study by Stigler and Friedland (1962), claiming that local regulation of electricity rates was ineffectual, is not consistent with those demand elasticities, since an unfettered monopolist would take advantage of low-elasticity demands and raise prices to levels at which demands were elastic. In contrast to that continued regulation of local monopolists, however, the Interstate Commerce Commission since the early 1980s has essentially abandoned shippers and recipients to the tender mercies of whichever railroad owns the siding or branch line that connects them to the main railroad network. See Winston et al. (1990) and Kwoka and White (1999).

94. See Pierce (1994). See Baumol and Sidak (1995) and Sidak and Spulber (1997) for discussions of stranded cost issues in that industry.

95. See, for example, *Brown Shoe Co. v. United States*, 370 U.S. 294 (1962).

96. For a historical interpretation of universal service in the U.S. telephone system, see Mueller (1997).

97. See, for example, Crandall and Waverman (1996).

98. Conceptually, that problem is not much different from the problem in figure 2-4 of a monopoly network *A* interacting with monopoly network *B*. Crandall and Waverman (1996) note that problem as well. One solution they suggest is that telephone subscribers be charged for incoming calls, which is currently done only for calls received by cellular telephones. That potential solution would involve a virtual revolution in the pricing structure of all other telephone services. Further, though charging for incoming calls would surely increase subscribers' sensitivities, it would not cure the fundamental problem: network externalities plus market power.

99. Interestingly, it is spectrum-based competition—from satellites—that may well provide cheap and effective competition for cable television. See Johnson (1994).

100. See Brennan (1995). That fiber-optic cable solution raises obvious problems of public provision, comparable to the public provision of roads that facilitates the competition that trucks provide to rail.

101. Trucks and roads could break or loosen the stranglehold of the local rail branch line and local marshaling yard, because

every sender and receiver of a truck shipment has easy access—a driveway or ramp—to the road network.

102. See Sherman (1980) and Sidak and Spulber (1996).

103. Casual empiricism with respect to comparisons of the U.S. telephone and electricity industries with their government-owned counterparts abroad supports that conclusion.

References

Artle, Roland, and Christian Averous. 1973. "The Telephone System as a Public Good: Static and Dynamic Aspects." *Bell Journal of Economics and Management Science* 4 (Spring): 89–100.

Averch, Harvey, and Leland L. Johnson. 1962. "Behavior of the Firm under Regulatory Constraint." *American Economic Review* 52: 1053–69.

Baron, David P. 1989. "Design of Regulatory Mechanisms and Institutions." Chap. 24 in *Handbook of Industrial Organization*, vol. 2, ed. Richard Schmalensee and Robert D. Willig. Amsterdam: North Holland.

Baumol, William J., and David F. Bradford. 1970. "Optimal Departures from Marginal Cost Pricing." *American Economic Review* 60 (June): 265–83.

Baumol, William J., and Alvin K. Klevorick. 1970. "Input Choices and Rate-of-Return Regulation: An Overview of the Discussion." *Bell Journal of Economics and Management Science* 1 (Autumn): 162–90.

Baumol, William J., and J. Gregory Sidak. 1994a. *Toward Competition in Local Telephony.* Cambridge and Washington, D.C.: MIT Press and AEI Press.

———. 1994b. "The Pricing of Inputs Sold to Competitors." *Yale Journal on Regulation* 11: 171–202.

———. 1995. *Transmission Pricing and Stranded Costs in the Electric Power Industry.* Washington, D.C.: AEI Press.

Besen, Stanley M., and Joseph Farrell. 1994. "Choosing How to Compete: Strategies and Tactics in Standardization." *Journal of Economic Perspectives* 8 (Spring): 117–31.

Besen, Stanley M., and Leland L. Johnson. 1986. *Compatibility Standards, Competition, and Innovation in the Broadcasting Industry.* Santa Monica, Calif.: RAND Corporation.

Braeutigam, Ronald R. 1989. "Optimal Policies for Natural Monopolies." Chap. 23 in *Handbook of Industrial Organization*, vol. 2, ed. Richard Schmalensee and Robert D. Willig. Amsterdam: North Holland.

Brennan, Timothy J. 1987. "Why Regulated Firms Should Be Kept out of Unregulated Markets: Understanding the Divestiture in *United States* v. *AT&T.*" *Antitrust Bulletin* 32 (Fall): 741–93.

———. 1990. "Cross-Subsidization and Cost Misallocation by Regulated Monopolists." *Journal of Regulatory Economics* 2 (March): 37–51.

———. 1995. "Is the Theory behind *U.S.* v. *AT&T* Applicable Today?" *Antitrust Bulletin* 40 (Fall): 455–82.

Brock, Gerald. 1994. *Telecommunication Policy for the Information Age: From Monopoly to Competition.* Cambridge: Harvard University Press.

Burton, Mark L. 1995. "Railroad Deregulation, Carrier Behavior, and Shipper Response: A Disaggregated Analysis." *Journal of Regulatory Economics* 5 (December): 417–34.

Burton, Mark L., and Wesley W. Wilson. 1995. "Network Pricing and Vertical Foreclosure in Railroad Markets." Mimeo, Department of Economics, University of Oregon (August).

Carlton, Dennis W., and Alan S. Frankel. 1995a. "The Antitrust Economics of Credit Card Networks." *Antitrust Law Journal* 63: 643–68.

———. 1995b. "The Antitrust Economics of Credit Card Networks: Reply to Evans and Schmalensee." *Antitrust Law Journal* 63: 903–15.

Carlton, Dennis W., and Steven C. Salop. 1996. "You Keep Knocking but You Can't Come in: Evaluating Restrictions on Access to Input Joint Ventures." *Harvard Journal of Law and Technology* 9: 319–52.

Caves, Richard E. 1962. *Air Transport and Its Regulators.* Cambridge: Harvard University Press.

Chamberlin, Edward H. 1956. *The Theory of Monopolistic Competition.* 7th ed. Cambridge: Harvard University Press.

Coase, Ronald. 1960. "The Problem of Social Cost." *Journal of Law and Economics* 3 (October): 1–44.

Cournot, Augustin. 1927. *Researches into the Mathematical Principles of the Theory of Wealth.* Translated by N. T. Bacon. New York: Macmillan (1838 original).

Crandall, Robert W. 1991. *After the Breakup: U.S. Telecommunications in a More Competitive Era.* Washington, D.C.: Brookings Institution.

Crandall, Robert W., and Leonard Waverman. 1996. *Talk Is Cheap: The Promise of Regulatory Reform in North American Telecommunications.* Washington, D.C.: Brookings Institution.

David, Paul, and Shane Greenstein. 1990. "The Economics of Compatibility Standards." *Economics of Innovation and New Technology* 1: 3–41.

Economides, Nicholas. 1996. "The Economics of Networks." *International Journal of Industrial Organization* 14 (October): 673–99.

Economides, Nicholas, and Charles Himmelberg. 1995. "Critical Mass and Network Evolution in Telecommunications." In *Toward a Competitive Telecommunication Industry*, ed. Gerald W. Brock. Mahwah, N.J.: Lawrence Erlbaum.

Economides, Nicholas, and Lawrence J. White. 1994. "Networks and Compatibility: Implications for Antitrust." *European Economic Review* 38 (April): 651–62.

———. 1995. "Access and Interconnection Pricing: How Efficient Is the 'Efficient Component Pricing Rule'?" *Antitrust Bulletin* 40 (Fall): 557–79.

———. 1998. "The Inefficiency of the ECPR Yet Again: A Reply." *Antitrust Bulletin* 43 (Summer): 429–44.

Evans, David S., ed. 1983. *Breaking up Bell: Essays on Industrial Organization and Regulation.* New York: North Holland.

Evans, David S., and Richard Schmalensee. 1995. "Economic Aspects of Payment Card Systems and Antitrust

Policy toward Joint Ventures." *Antitrust Law Journal* 65: 861–902.

———. 1999. "Joint Venture Membership: Visa and Discover Card (1993)." In *The Antitrust Revolution: Economics, Competition, and Policy*, 3d ed., ed. John E. Kwoka, Jr., and Lawrence J. White. New York: Oxford University Press.

Farrell, Joseph, and Garth Saloner. 1985. "Standardization, Compatibility, and Innovation." *RAND Journal of Economics* 16 (Spring): 70–86.

———. 1986. "Installed Base and Compatibility: Innovation, Product Preannouncement, and Predation." *American Economic Review* 76 (December): 940–55.

Friedlaender, Ann F. 1969. *The Dilemma of Freight Transport Regulation*. Washington, D.C.: Brookings Institution.

Friedlaender, Ann F., and Richard H. Spady. 1981. *Freight Transport Regulation: Equity, Efficiency, and Competition in the Rail and Trucking Industries*. Cambridge: MIT Press.

Grimm, Curtis M., Clifford Winston, and Carol S. Evans. 1992. "Foreclosure of Railroad Markets: A Test of Chicago Leverage Theory." *Journal of Law and Economics* 35 (October): 295–310.

Guerin-Calvert, Margaret E. 1994. "Vertical Integration as a Threat to Competition: Airline Computer Reservation Systems." In *The Antitrust Revolution: The Role of Economics*, 2d ed., ed. John E. Kwoka , Jr., and Lawrence J. White. New York: HarperCollins.

Guerin-Calvert, Margaret E., and Steven S. Wildman. 1991. *Electronic Services Networks: A Business and Public Policy Challenge*. New York: Praeger.

Hausman, Jerry A., and Timothy J. Tardiff. 1995. "Efficient Local Exchange Competition." *Antitrust Bulletin* 40 (Fall): 529–56.

Hazlett, Thomas W., and Matthew L. Spitzer. 1997. *Public Policy toward Cable Television: The Economics of Rate Controls*. Cambridge and Washington, D.C.: MIT Press and AEI Press.

Johnson, Leland L. 1994. *Toward Competition in Cable Television*. Cambridge and Washington, D.C.: MIT Press and AEI Press.

Joskow, Paul L., and Roger G. Noll. 1994. "Economic Regulation: Deregulation and Regulatory Reform during the 1980s." In *American Economic Policy in the 1980s*, ed. Martin Feldstein. Chicago: University of Chicago Press.

Joskow, Paul L., and Nancy L. Rose. 1989. "The Effects of Economic Regulation." Chap. 25 in *Handbook of Industrial Organization*, vol. 2, ed. Richard Schmalensee and Robert D. Willig. Amsterdam: North Holland.

Joskow, Paul L., and Richard Schmalensee. 1983. *Markets for Power: An Analysis of Electrical Utility Deregulation*. Cambridge: MIT Press.

Katz, Michael L., and Carl Shapiro. 1986. "Technology Adoption in the Presence of Network Externalities." *Journal of Political Economy* 94: 822–41.

———. 1994. "Systems Competition and Network Effects." *Journal of Economic Perspectives* 8 (Spring): 93–115.

Krueger, Anne O. 1974. "The Political Economy of the Rent-Seeking Society." *American Economic Review* 66 (June): 291–303.

Kwoka, John E., Jr., and Lawrence J. White. 1999. "Market Destiny?: The Union Pacific and Southern Pacific Railroad Merger." In *The Antitrust Revolution: Economics, Competition, and Policy*, 3d ed., ed. John E. Kwoka, Jr., and Lawrence J. White. New York: Oxford University Press.

Laffont, Jean-Jacques, and Jean Tirole. 1993. *A Theory of Incentives in Procurement and Regulation*. Cambridge: MIT Press.

Lewis, Lucinda M., and Robert J. Reynolds. 1979. "Appraising Alternatives to Regulation for Natural Monopolies." In *Oil Pipelines and Public Policy*, ed. Edward J. Mitchell. Washington, D.C.: American Enterprise Institute.

Liebowitz, S. J., and Stephen E. Margolis. 1994. "Network Externality: An Uncommon Tragedy." *Journal of Economic Perspectives* 8 (Spring): 133–50.

Lopatka, John E., and Joseph J. Simons. 1991. "Real Estate Multiple Listing Services and Antitrust Revisited." In *Electronic Services Networks: A Business and Public Policy Challenge*, ed. Margaret E. Guerin-Calvert and Steven S. Wildman. New York: Praeger.

MacAvoy, Paul W. 1983. *Energy Policy: An Economic Analysis.* New York: Norton.

———. 1996. *The Failure of Antitrust and Regulation to Establish Competition in Long-Distance Telephone Services.* Cambridge and Washington, D.C.: MIT Press and AEI Press.

MacAvoy, Paul W., and James Sloss. 1967. *Regulation of Transport Innovation: The ICC and Unit Coal Trains to the East Coast.* New York: Random House.

MacDonald, James M. 1989. "Railroad Deregulation, Innovation, and Competition: Effects of the Staggers Act on Grain Transportation." *Journal of Law and Economics* 32 (April): 63–95.

McFarland, Henry. 1989. "The Effects of United States Railroad Deregulation on Shippers, Labor, and Capital." *Journal of Regulatory Economics* 1 (September): 259–70.

Meyer, John R., Merton J. Peck, John Stenason, and Charles Zwick. 1959. *The Economics of Competition in the Transportation Industries.* Cambridge: Harvard University Press.

Moore, Thomas G. 1986. "Rail and Trucking Deregulation." In *Regulatory Reform: What Actually Happened,* ed. Leonard W. Weiss and Michael Klass. Boston: Little, Brown.

Morrison, Stephen, and Clifford Winston. 1986. *The Economic Effects of Airline Deregulation.* Washington, D.C.: Brookings Institution.

Mueller, Milton L., Jr. 1997. *Universal Service: Competition, Interconnection, and Monopoly in the Making of the American Telephone System.* Cambridge and Washington, D.C.: MIT Press and AEI Press.

Noll, Roger G. 1989. "Economic Perspectives on the Politics of Regulation." Chap. 22 in *Handbook of Industrial Organization,* vol. 2, ed. Richard Schmalensee and Robert D. Willig. Amsterdam: North Holland.

Noll, Roger G., and Bruce M. Owen. 1994. "The Anticompetitive Uses of Regulation: *United States* v. *AT&T* (1982)." In *The Antitrust Revolution: The Role of Economics,* 2d ed., ed. John E. Kwoka, Jr., and Lawrence J. White. New York: HarperCollins.

Owen, Bruce M., and Paul D. Gottlieb. 1986. "The Rise and Fall and Rise of Cable Television Regulation." In

Regulatory Reform: What Actually Happened, ed. Leonard W. Weiss and Michael W. Klass. Boston: Little, Brown.

Peltzman, Sam. 1976. "Toward a More General Theory of Regulation." *Journal of Law and Economics* 19 (August): 211–40.

Pierce, Richard J. 1994. "The State of the Transition to Competitive Markets in Natural Gas and Electricity." *Energy Law Journal* 15: 323–50.

Port Authority of New York and New Jersey. 1999. *Airport Flight Guide, January 1, 1999–March 31, 1999.*

Posner, Richard A. 1971. "Taxation by Regulation." *Bell Journal of Economics and Management Science* 2 (Spring): 22–50.

———. 1974. "Theories of Economic Regulation." *Bell Journal of Economics and Management Science* 5 (Autumn): 335–58.

Ratner, James. 1988. "Should There Be an Essential Facilities Doctrine?" *University of California, Davis, Law Review* 21: 327–82.

Reiffen, David, and Andrew N. Kleit. 1990. "Terminal Railroad Revisited: Foreclosure of an Essential Facility or Simply Horizontal Monopoly?" *Journal of Law and Economics* 33 (October): 419–38.

Rohlfs, Jeffrey. 1974. "A Theory of Interdependent Demand for a Communications Service." *Bell Journal of Economics and Management Science* 5 (Spring): 16–37.

Sappington, David E. M., and David S. Sibley. 1992. "Strategic Nonlinear Pricing under Price-Cap Regulation." *RAND Journal of Economics* 23 (Spring): 1–19.

Sappington, David E. M., and Dennis L. Weisman. 1996. *Designing Incentive Regulation for the Telecommunications Industry.* Cambridge and Washington, D.C.: MIT Press and AEI Press.

Sherman, Roger, ed. 1980. *Perspectives on Postal Service Issues.* Washington, D.C.: American Enterprise Institute.

Sidak, J. Gregory, and Daniel F. Spulber. 1996. *Protecting Competition from the Postal Monopoly.* Washington, D.C.: AEI Press.

———. 1997. *Deregulatory Takings and the Regulatory Contract: The Competitive Transformation of Network Industries in the United States.* New York: Cambridge University Press.

Stigler, George J. 1971. "The Theory of Regulation." *Bell Journal of Economics and Management Science* 2 (Spring): 3–21.

Stigler, George J., and Claire Friedland. 1962. "What Can Regulators Regulate? The Case of Electricity." *Journal of Law and Economics* 5 (October): 1–16.

Stover, John F. 1961. *American Railroads.* Chicago: University of Chicago Press.

Taylor, Lester D. 1994. *Telecommunications Demand in Theory and Practice.* Amsterdam: Kluwer Academic.

Teske, Paul, Samuel Best, and Michael Mintrom. 1995. *Deregulating Freight Transportation: Delivering the Goods.* Washington, D.C.: AEI Press.

Vogelsang, Ingo, and Bridger M. Mitchell. 1997. *Telecommunications Competition: The Last Ten Miles.* Cambridge and Washington, D.C.: MIT Press and AEI Press.

Weisman, Dennis L. 1993. "Superior Regulatory Regimes in Theory and Practice." *Journal of Regulatory Economics* 5 (December): 355–66.

———. 1994. "Why Less May Be More under Price-Cap Regulation." *Journal of Regulatory Economics* 6 (December): 339–61.

Werden, Gregory. 1988. "The Law and Economics of the Essential Facilities Doctrine." *St. Louis University Law Review* 32: 432–80.

White, Lawrence J. 1972. "Quality Variation When Prices Are Regulated." *Bell Journal of Economics and Management Science* 3 (Autumn): 425–36.

———. 1975. "Quality, Competition, and Regulation: Evidence from the Airline Industry." In *Regulating the Product: Quality and Variety,* ed. Richard E. Caves and Marc J. Roberts. Cambridge: Ballinger.

———. 1991. *The S&L Debacle: Public Policy Lessons for Bank and Thrift Regulation.* New York: Oxford University Press.

———. 1993a. "A Cautionary Tale of Deregulation Gone Awry: The S&L Debacle." *Southern Economic Journal* 59 (January): 496–514.

————. 1993b. "The Community Reinvestment Act: Good Intentions Headed in the Wrong Direction." *Fordham Urban Law Journal* 20 (Winter): 281–92.

————. 1993c. "Competition Policy in the United States: An Overview." *Oxford Review of Economic Policy* 9 (Summer): 133–53.

————. 1994. "Market Failures, Government Failures, and Economic Development." Working Paper #EC-94-02, Department of Economics, Stern School of Business, New York University.

Wilson, Wesley W. 1994. "Market-Specific Effects of Rail Deregulation." *Journal of Industrial Economics* (March): 1–22.

Winston, Clifford. 1993. "Economic Deregulation: Days of Reckoning for Microeconomists." *Journal of Economic Literature* 31 (September): 1263–89.

Winston, Clifford, Thomas M. Corsi, Curtis M. Grimm, and Carol A. Evans. 1990. *The Economic Effects of Surface Freight Deregulation.* Washington, D.C.: Brookings Institution.

Wolf, Charles, Jr. 1989. *Markets or Governments: Choosing between Imperfect Alternatives.* Cambridge: MIT Press.

About the Author

LAWRENCE J. WHITE is the Arthur E. Imperatore Professor of Economics at New York University's Stern School of Business. He has served as a senior staff economist at the Council of Economic Advisers, as director of the Economic Policy Office in the Antitrust Division of the U.S. Department of Justice, and as a member of the Federal Home Loan Bank Board. He is the author of many books, including *The S&L Debacle: Public Policy Lessons for Bank and Thrift Regulation* (Oxford University Press, 1991), and was the North American editor of the *Journal of Industrial Economics,* 1984–1987 and 1990–1995.

J O I N T C E N T E R

AEI-BROOKINGS JOINT CENTER FOR REGULATORY STUDIES

In response to growing concerns about understanding the impact of regulation on consumers, business, and government, the American Enterprise Institute and the Brookings Institution have established the new AEI-Brookings Joint Center for Regulatory Studies. The primary purpose of the center is to hold lawmakers and regulators more accountable by providing thoughtful, objective analysis of existing regulatory programs and new regulatory proposals. The Joint Center will build on AEI's and Brookings's impressive body of work over the past three decades that has evaluated the economic impact of regulation and offered constructive suggestions for implementing reforms to enhance productivity and consumer welfare. The views in Joint Center publications are those of the authors and do not necessarily reflect the views of the staff, council of academic advisers, or fellows.

COUNCIL OF ACADEMIC ADVISERS